'Dakota Feirer is a poet of great skill. Each work in this collection is a song, every line a layer of our sense of selves as Mob. Feirer is also a poet who respects those who have walked and written before him. I know this through his words.'
TONY BIRCH

'*Arsenic Flower* carves meaning from masculinity and memory. Tender and intimate . . . It's a healing expression of contemporary blak masculinity'
BOOKS + PUBLISHING

'Exquisite, profound and deeply moving'
VOGUE AUSTRALIA

Dakota Feirer is a First Nations Australian (Bundjalung and Gumbaynggirr) storyteller with work published in *Overland* literary journal, *Wonderground* journal, *Rabbit Poetry* and *Australian Poetry*. His work consists of poems, prose and spoken word performances that engage with Country, culture, resurgence and manhood. Dakota believes in healing Country and our communities through art and storytelling.

ARSENIC FLOWER

DAKOTA FEIRER

Published in Australia and New Zealand in 2025
by Hachette Australia
(an imprint of Hachette Australia Pty Limited)
Gadigal Country, Level 17, 207 Kent Street, Sydney, NSW 2000
www.hachette.com.au

Hachette Australia acknowledges and pays our respects to the past and present Traditional Owners and Custodians of Country throughout Australia and recognises the continuation of cultural, spiritual and educational practices of Aboriginal and Torres Strait Islander peoples. Our head office is located on the lands of the Gadigal people of the Eora Nation.

Copyright © Dakota Feirer 2025

This book is copyright. Apart from any fair dealing for the purposes of private study, research, criticism or review permitted under the *Copyright Act 1968*, no part may be stored or reproduced by any process without prior written permission. Enquiries should be made to the publisher.

 A catalogue record for this book is available from the National Library of Australia

ISBN: 978 0 7336 5363 6 (paperback)

Cover design by Alex Ross
Cover artwork courtesy of Charlotte Allingham (charlotteallingham.com)
Author photograph courtesy of Anna Holman
Typeset in 12/16.5 pt Bembo MT Pro by Bookhouse, Sydney

For Mum and Dad.

For the flowers.

For the soil.

Contents

Seed   1

    Boy   3
    Heal Country   4
    Death by Vertigo   6
    NEVILLE'S QUANTUM THEORY   10
    Crown   11
    Spear I   13
    SHE   15
    1966   16
    SS14   18
    Arsenic Muse   22
    WRONG SKIN   25
    trees leaves solemnity   27
    WATER & SMOKE   30

Pollen   35

    she-oaked shores   37
    Brachychiton acerifolius   39
    Shadow Coast   41
    A Blanket for Oberon   43

Wamban Woman	45
Goori Horse Whispering	47
Tracker's Eyes	48
butterflies	50
Moral Frontier I	51
Moral Frontier II	53
Arsenic Itinerary	55

Soil   59

Spear II	61
The Bawden Lectures I	62
The Bawden Lectures II	64
The Bawden Lectures III	66
The Bawden Lectures IV	67
The Bawden Lectures V	69
Daam Miirlarl	70

Root   71

Rise	73
There's Medicine in the Ashes	74
Old Man's Legacy	77
Corners	78
runaway	79
Blood Cedar Dreams	80

Sandon Point Theory   82
Shield   83
Aboard a Booing-37   84
A Bowerbird for Warrawong   85
Arsenic Flower   87

Song   91

Easy-Bake Reconciliation Cupcakes (makes 12)   93
Spear III   95
Nature Feels   96
25-to-life-type-dedication   99
consult to me   102
Change Direction   105
Dreams   107
fishing net   108
Cedar Creek   110

Rain   111

still coffee   113
Old Mogo Town I   115
Old Mogo Town II   117
Hunter-Gatherer   120
Opal   122
Cowboys Don't Cry   124

empty pegs	127
empty pegs II	129
I am	132
Spear IV	134

Notes   135

Acknowledgements   149

Seed

Boy

to the boy
who climbed
the tree
to see
the world

Heal Country

If I wrote a letter to my Country, how would it read?

Dear *Bundjalung Jugun* / Dear *Yuwinj Dhari*

>   Will you forgive the infidelity of the Anthropocene?
>   Because it took too many ancestors before my arrival
>
>   I know this truth, no new philosophy
>   though I'm growing tired of repeating the words
>
>   *Heal Country.*
>
>   Days have gone by and the words still echo
>   a proud 3% of your attention
>   yet we still linger   like good echoes
>   'til the next blak theme paints our screens and guernseys
>
>   *Heal Country.*
>
>   I know wisdom belongs not to me
>   but to the man that plants a tree
>   whose shade he'll never sit underneath
>
>   *Heal Country.*

Where wisdom made me there's a ceremony ground
piling with dead leaves. So much, I lit a cultural fire
    by my porch
so my feet wouldn't bleed. If this colony is a house
its doorstep is where I sleep.

I keep checking its mailbox to find this letter to my
    Country

stamped in red ink:

    Return to Sender.

So, maybe I'll just print my heart on this letter

stamped in red ochre:

    Return to Ancestor.

Death by Vertigo

The Killing Times Have Ended
so say the books I've read.

Through windows watched
apocalypse, recorded
moments in social posts.

Until glass cracked like
country roads and melted
like highway signposts.

A child's eyes bathed
in wildfire grows
fear in adult
minds.

Scrolling through our
species undeserving
of love or virality.

Unlearning their
true story, yearning
to be sung again.

Information becomes
an abyss of numbness.
Carted around in
pockets.

Our care now also
dwindles. On cliff
edge of news
fatigue.

Joining the
livestream of
endangered
species.

Desacralised in a
thirsting ember of shorthand
violence – media cycles.

Burnt
carcasses
wired on our
coat of
arms.

Our totems
wailing, those

>   unburnt lost in
>   haze.
>
>   Anthro-gaze
>   is failing
>   generations
>   depending on us.

The unborn pleading:

> *Please stop her bleeding.*
>
> *Please tend to*
> *bandaging your*
> *nationhood's*
> *fragility.*
>
> *Please consider our*
> *inheritance, our soon*
> *lifeless Country.*

To heal a corrupt legacy,
we weave with finger and reed.

Baskets, hands, poetry, opinion
piece. Listen. Breathe. Firestick.
Drying leaves.

Through
necessity we
must re-
member.

Rematriate
our love for
our Mother.

Deradicalise love crimes,
like protecting birthing trees.

Learn the plight of our totems.
Listen to mountains and streams.

The Killing Times Are Of The Past,
so the journos have said.

Distrusting them, I consult the stars:

when will the birthing times commence?

NEVILLE'S QUANTUM THEORY

Solve to CALCULATE YOUR CASTE *from the following formulae* (25 marks):

$$\sqrt{spear} + aboriginal\ flag \div 1788 = x$$

$$\frac{gumleaves}{bushfires} \div (smoking\ ceremony)^{Naidoc\ Week} + shake\ a\ leg \times welcome^2(country) = \$x$$

$$^{reconciliation}\sqrt{referundum} = x$$

$$Rabbit\ Proof\ Fence\ (RPF) = \sqrt{January(26) + x}$$

$$\frac{coffee}{milk} = still\ coffee > x\%(aboriginality)$$

$$\begin{pmatrix} RPF & \cdots & 1967 \\ \vdots & \ddots & \vdots \\ 2023 & \cdots & RAP \end{pmatrix}$$

$$\frac{B\textrm{Ł}óò\textrm{Ḍ}}{x} \times \sqrt{∀.Ø.\textrm{Ň}ΣV\textrm{ï}\textrm{Ł}\textrm{L}·\textrm{ê}} = \mathscr{G} \mp \infty$$

Show your working.

Crown
– *for Byron*

STONE PLATEAUS STAGED MANY GREAT WARS
SUCH WARS ECHO & PLATEAUS REMEMBER

MANY STOOD ACROSS STONE & FOUGHT
OVER PRIDE, TERRITORY, CROWNS OF A SORT

ECHOES STILL LINGER
OF TWO GREAT SOLDIERS

WHO STOOD PROUD & PRODIGAL
ON ANCESTRAL SHOULDERS

THEIR VALIANT CAMPAIGNS
SPRAWLED TIME AND SOIL

SEVERING THEIR CHAINS
THEY ASCENDED AS ROYALS

THE WAR DISPLACED THEM
TWO CENTURIES NORTH

SO THEIR BATTLES TOOK PLACE
ACROSS HANDBALL COURTS

SUCH BECAME OF THEIR OLD PLATEAUS
CHURNED INTO MORTAR IN THE DISTANT NORTH

EACH RECESS THEY LEARNT OF WAR'S ENDLESSNESS
CONQUERING IN THE ART OF THE SPHERICAL SWORD

THE SQUARED LOOP
THE FRONTIER ANEW

EVERY VICTORY OF OURS
WAS WON ON THEIR GROUNDS

EVEN IF IT WAS
THE ONLY CROWN WE WERE ALLOWED

Spear I

Be the Spear
an old man once said.

A saying passed down with soft hands to sons
                                              and
                                              grandsons.

Hold your Spear with back straight and chin high
in service to the stories from the sky.

Exist not under shelter from the world
but stand in the rain.

Cast your spirit to the stars
become a student of sacrifice, silence & solitude.

Seek emphasis on self-love, self-esteem, self-work
whether seen or not seen.

Should you ever stall in the dark
be it only to stalk your deepest shadows.

To be the spear,
submit to your benign spirit.

Tend to love as a stream amidst the cosmos
understand its touch: a sacred place of creation.

Be a sentry for the balance of the universe
a shield for all that is sacred.

Stand strong like warrior
speak soft like the stars.

Be the Spear, my son
an old man once said.

SHE

each full moon

the ocean takes home more of her shells   dissolving
histories from man
who wanes from the sacred

land back starts with washing hands and washing hearts
clean

where sweet water creek meets saltwater kiss of sea
                        whirlpools dance with urgency

full moon has come
none, as sovereign as she.

1966
— *for Dad*

I

blak boy is born / with a mouthful / of silence
blak boy is taught / to hold posture / wrists outward
blak boy meets world / yet to referendum him / blak or boy
so blak boy cedes words / for a sovereignty of silence
blak boy yearns / from terraced edges of redfern
patient blak boy works / scratching pockets at the block until
blak boy met molasses / on horseback his heart changed axis

II

blak boy dreamt and longed / for a land far and beyond
surveying greener edges / he traded terrace for wire fences
where blak boy found a place / with pastoral name and creek line
ceding skin for leather / finding warmth at storms' horizons
he rode horses in the rain / and left the boy behind
until he met himself / in his firstborn's silent eyes

III

blak boy meets world / yet to referendum him / a voice
so patience blak boy learns / from the fringes of a storm
blak boy holds a spear / from father's shoulders he could reach
blak boy fears his pain / sculpting his tightened fists
blak boy stands in the rain / a sovereign shape of universe
where blak boy cedes not words / but colours them / with story
here every blak boy is born / with a mouthful / of memory

SS14

bleeding static crackles across an interstellar radio. incoming message follows

KRXSHHH ... GOOD MORNING ALL CADETS, PLEASE REPORT TO YOUR STATIONS FOR YOUR DAILY BRIEFIN ... SHHHKRXSHH ... IT HAS BEEN APPROX 250 LIGHTYEARS ABOARD THE MIGHTY SS14, SINCE DEARLY DEPARTING OUR MOTHER EARTH FOR OUR ASSIMILATION-MISSION FOR HUMANITY *ARSENIC FLOWE* ... KRSHHH ... SSZIP.

message concluded. radio silence

Pretty girl smiles your way   *act fast*
sweep the hair from your eyes   *don't stumble*
hide that gap inyourteeth and   *inyourself*
let her know your proudest wonder   *your ancestry.*

Her smile less wondrous, ponders idly
on A.O. parallel timeline she recites:

"SO, WHERE DO YOU STAND . . . ON NEVILLE'S QUANTUM THEORY?"

Tireless, dreaded theorem
morning microdose of PTSD
fist clenched, invisible spear fastened
                        ready.
Abdomen flexed, burying noxiousness
acquired from dimension walking?
Or caused by the casualness –
how the words flow, from juvenile lips.

On your original timeline
her question echoes:

"So what, you're part abo?"

Like icebergs
               hide them deep.

Nullify tells of an internal screaming mess
field that bead of sweat
falling from flowering arsenic armpit
before you collapse   in the summerness
between the gaps   adolescence and biceps
bite your tongue, that now shapes a speartip
search for an escape pod on A.O.'s spaceship:

CADET, OR NOT – THIS IS NO PLACE
FOR THOSE OF YOUR UNFORTUNATE CONSCRIPT

Prettiness melting, the hot girls' jury chime in:

"Summer school's expensive –
you on a 'black' scholarship?"

Grip the collar of your shirt so it doesn't stick
cotton drapes over teenage shoulders heavier than usual
thick, though it is still not armour
numbness, more rather.

        Am I / are you a warrior still?

As if my / *our* compromise were not enough
leaving mother, home, Country – all behind.

Stripped naked, suspended, animated
    – lynched on the other side of history
by an A.O. Neville Quantum theorem.

I am numb to this abyss
in all its pretty girls and questions.

The son of the tortured mother grows aggressive

yet *anger* my mother condemned, so to bend black temper
into the colour of imagination — a jaded cosmic escape.

I suck my teeth. Wince to the floor.

Quickdraw my portal gun, from rear skinny jean holster —

> KRXSHHH . . . CADET
> YOU'VE RECEIVED A MESSAGE FROM
> MOTHER EART . . . SHHHKRXSHH . . .

Mum texts:

"How's day one my son?"

Once more, I laugh sarcastically
while adjusting my balls, just as casually
hiding my gaps

> *my hidden plea for mercy.*

Arsenic Muse

I see chaos resting on your heart lately.

Undressed you are
flying fluorescently
drinking from their gaze.

Bathing in applause
of clicking fingers
pouring of love-lost-missionary lust.

I see you through the chaos; that is
the lip-biting, gin-sinking
sand-swept blonde shadows.

Licking their teeth
at your shirt;
running out of buttons.

You are the son of leather
and I see chaos spread across your hips.

Gripping your belt, I see
acrylic fingertips.

Cashless tapping land tax
shameless reconciliation.

Kiss the gloss and guilt
from their apologetic lips
hard and bespoke like you know.

I see your heart; albeit its chaos.

Quite a moonlit,
half-cut, allegorical
smile you have.

Standing in the flame of your art
skin is burning
yet still smirking
you're still dancing in the dark.

I see what turns the pages
of poetry on your chest.

You are the son of a tortured mother
and this chaos is a muse to you.

I see your heart dancing by itself
a self-condoned pain, they're clicking too.

This muse has you
dubious amidst the stars
and will be your final arch, I see.

If your feet can't find the soil first
your chest will spell arsenic
and resting upon it

— empty dirt, I see.

WRONG SKIN

I've been hiding my tears
from my grandmother for years.

Couldn't tell her
I hated the colour
of my bathroom mirror.

Detached from a complexion
reflecting someone other than me.
Silently screaming, crying
closing-the-gap
in-my-teeth.

Wrong-skin trapped in the mirror
marked heavily with black ink.

Recalling the dark places I've been
are old fingertips and tattoos, together they
trace my shadow-home, together they
grace a quantum-chrome, together they
mourn the colour   of my grandmother.

For years hidden tears
filled my bathroom sink.
    In hopes old hands

may wash this skin
with clay and wrists and river.

Unhinged from shame one day
– I painted my body
stripes of river and clay
head-banded standing
a proud-flowering-beautiful.

Chanting sacred song and dance
holding hands with my pride.

Together they dance
              – shadows, tattoos, fingertips
a moonlit chrome and kin
Grandmother forgive my tears and my ink
for I have been –
              learning to love
              through song
              my mirror and my wrong skin.

trees leaves solemnity

three green oak trees lined the street across from my
balcony
that same place she first handed her cigarette to me
still imprinted with her dark red lipstick
knowing I would eventually taste it
along with that flavour of cheap red wine
that night I was hers and she was mine
a love endowed and governed through time

day by day, outside grows colder
the trees' leaves change colour and start to wander
day by day, our hearts grow fonder
though eventually, the falling leaves dance like ghosts in
the street
like diligent thieves, they stole her away from me

now all I know is
solemnity
and all I see are
trees with no *leaves*

it's been months and I'm still feelin less like me
been smokin more than usual and can't stop listening
to R'n'B

sleepin is never easy
haunted by dreams and memories of histories

histories of magic, romance and ancestry
histories where real men were born from matriarchies

but I wake up to a
deep-voiced lost boy
forced to live in a heteropatriarchy

still feel it in my dreams, the horror
thrown in chains by foreign names
forced a discourse that says: emotional pain does not
equate to a strong male

I guess a teardrop cannot travel through a suit of
chainmail
probably had ancestors that wore that shit
probably turn in their graves after hearing all of this.

what choice does
a deep-voiced lost boy have?

fuckboys don't cry
fuckboys lie
fuckboys don't even have a heart inside

so then I asked why?

why is it when she left it killed me
but I only wished I had died
that way I wouldn't have realised

that pain travels in circles
and never in straight lines

if I was born long before – as a real man
I would build you a house full of sunlight
with no glass ceilings
and you could surpass my success
without damaging my feelings

I still wrestle with the words
man
and
meaning
in the so-called 21st century

now I can barely stand tall in sight

so I threw away my spine

now every kiss tastes like spite

doused in cheap red wine

WATER & SMOKE
– *for the land of the five islands*

Them days we spent pouring melancholy
into her freshwater veins
atop creek bed, drawing crooked vanity
in the push and pull of her breath.

Spilling our names into flames and coolamon
resting fulfilled, emptying
lungs of water and smoke
we were healing.

Facing east in eulogy
at the end of the world
above whitewash
and below westwind.

Old caretakers sit still in-circle
with hands woven from stories
they gesture you to come near
and return to stirring black tea
and whispers.

The cadence of your heartbeat
suffices for introduction.

Stoking flames beside end's doorway
their looks are language without voice
that growl:
> *See here and now*
> *keep our fire going*
> *keep our river flowing.*
> *Because in the end*
> *the world will need*
> *water and smoke.*

Let twilight flood your eyelids.

Ponder days of Kuradgi
ancients who wandered shadows
dunes now long faded

From ochre tomb who rose in wonder
of what so-called-progress has incurred
upon this promised womb.

If Kuradgi could see here and now
from stone plateau. Eroding conditions
of middens for the sake of our coal coast.

What song he would sing
what smoke and ceremony he would bring.

Smoke like ochre flows between matter.
Between solid, liquid and gas is where spirit resides.

Outside the binds of western isms
lives the Lore of water and smoke.

Smoke like culture reminds to move
with conviction: between matter.
Between the magnificence of presence
and what actually doesn't matter.

Catharsis is creation
an invisible currency between the world
and you.

Igniting it with every breath.
This is where we arrive at progress.
Should it be – a cathartic pursuit.
Though *here* and *now* are misconstrued as commodities.
Progress worn around temporal-bound wrists
working as mercenaries to ego and greed
fighting for cheques 'til the death and drowning
blindly meandering from a sorrowful mother.

Making sandcastles of our minerals
our knowledge, our bones.

What an apocalypse
this so-called-progress is.

What will be new
in a world of broken songlines?
Here and now we rise, and reassess.
To nurture home for those who come next.

Because in the end
we'll all return to a womb
made from Country.

We'd like it if you'd join us
above whitewash and below westwind
for some black tea and whispers.

As long as before you leave this world:
> *Keep that fire going*
> *and keep that river flowing.*
> *Because the world needs*
> *water and smoke.*

Pollen

she-oaked shores

Somewhere in between beginning and end
are shaded beds on sacred bends
made in layers of leaves resembling strands of ancient
sacred ladies.

Where sweet waters ebb, and soft northern winds blow
Faceless Maidens bellow, my arms and Nawi follow
as their rhythms sing me home, upriver.

Here
spirits creep amongst echoes.

Keep dry eyes on sweet water's tides, watch them rise,
 before I fall.
For saltier waters dissolve river borders, for once, stay on
 course.
In branches, old lore women call, guiding my oars
 toward she-oaked shores.

Wrinkled bark mimics brown skin, carved marks reveal
 maps of kinship
names, voices and stories all told in sacred song
and Grandmothers of she-oak, hold sacred bends strong.

Singing recedes from the tips of her scale leaves
down to a humming heartbeat in the earth
beneath my feet.

Grandest mother, I'm sorry
we never had a chance to meet
I'm sorry your roots are far deeper than mine.

For now, I hope this bed of tears will suffice
so swallow me at the end of every apology
and embrace my body, in the roots of casuarina.

Melodic medicinal symphony of timeless ancestress
my name has been sung here for eternity
my name has been sung by her, for eternity
she-oak, she-knows, what is done and yet to come.

Earthen maternal sounds of her soft wind song
sing me into the ground
upriver, where my bones belong.

Brachychiton acerifolius

Brachychiton acerifolius		
habitNotes		
"A red-flowering Kurrajong. Sergeant Clark writes:	seeds from this tree have been sown on many occasions but	. . . there from invariably produces a white flower."
recordedBy		
Bloodstained pages frame	rules of	an imperial game
embroidered	emboldened	embellished
executioners knighted by	'ologists	precious appellatives.
family		
Each stroke	of ink	on paper
equals	imperial	salutation
deepening	scars	on sacred land and paperbarks.
habitat		
Though true	depth is absent	from inkpot.
Buoying	a royal	crown
above the deepest	ocean	of stories.

	genus	
Deified	authorities	waltzing matilda
through their	curated gardens	of stolen knowledge
falsehoods	dancing above	a terra nullius.
	scientificName	
Botany has	both raped and erased	your flame
stifled	your	beauty
POISON	marks	your name now.
	specificEpithet	
Under the guise	of a blind Latin	tongue
seeds and leaves	crushed between leather	of boot and journal
now mere shadows	pressed	across spreadsheet.
	notes	
songlines are no less dismembered beyond these cells *roots thread deeper than introduced infrastructure* *belly holds water while hands bleed rivers* *holding memory and babies* *women's business tree.*		

Shadow Coast
– *for Tahnee*

blissful embrace from billabong fleece
to end a twilight dance with autumn oceans

slipping head and arms into sleeves
still holding a fallen sunset

resting on these shoulders
long days dissolve into oceans

and we could be so still
that shadows turn to greet us

our textures embrace
a grandiose love note
spelling *early autumn lover water*

rummaging the bottom of billabong pockets
sliding silver onto fingers unbothered
by grinding shrapnel of sand and shell and history

coursing our ambiguous skin
waters stirring medicine
something old still dancing

sun-bleached curls and corduroy to match
fleece and macramé and tattooed toes
and keep-cup and home-job shit-chops

ocean keeper's grandchildren
we survived the shadows of time
by wearing the colour of our shells

to be held by these arms
of sun and shadows and ocean
must have a word of its own

A Blanket for Oberon

you built a nest in the clouds, high country, Wiradjuri
neighbouring the smell you could taste
of the old sawmill and winters that held
whispers to histories of blood, frost, industry

where dogs ran adrift from domestic nature
and horses went to die.
a tractor lay in eternal slumber
in a rusted archive of pastoral shed

time wove together differently
in your remote cloudy nest
or so it felt for winters we'd spend
up in the high country

your coffee-wrinkled hands would tuck me in
your voice rolling down your fingertips
smoothing layers of blankets
you wrapped me in them with your stories

pointing through the window, you told me

pick a star

so my eyes wandered the Oberon sky

tomorrow . . .
you look for that same star

in my search, I'd learn to love them all
from the warmth of your fingertips and stories and
blankets woven from timeless threads
of every one of our grandmothers' nests

Wamban Woman

I tried to picture
the colour of your eyes
sinking when I realised –
I could not recall them.

That I could be so selfish
to not have engraved them
into the silhouette
of you in my head.

As if I could forget, the colour
of grace,
of selflessness,
of soothing wind,
soft autumn mist,
of morning stars
and warming presence.

As if I could forget, the colour
that attended my first breath.
Or the way they glisten
when you mourn the boy who grew old and left.

So in my next glance in Wamban:
I'll gather the medicine from them.
So I may paint my memories
in the colour of ancient shale and riverbed.

Goori Horse Whispering

The shudder of the shoulder

                you taught me to sense.

The direction of the ears, eyes blinking

                      you taught me to see.

The drop of the head
licking and chewing
a wet grindstone like

now
      son
            join-up

Tracker's Eyes

Some stories are of salvation
told to soften the hearts of our babies.

Some stories tell how Tracker chased famous murderers
how he track'em up rusty river banks where the ghosts
of the murdered would point out their own graves.

Some stories blur the lines
like woven vines of black and blue
assured the police had trust in their Tracker
recovering many a corpse at the end of his pointer finger.

If I had inherited his eyes
his gifts – his sight
if I could see the future or the past
untangle the whispering vines
for years that flowed downriver.

Other stories just make sense later
as our hearts learn the family calluses
hardened from walking
Grafton's gravel roads.

Some stories petrify against the grain of time
spilling into the hearts of our babies

through the cracks   we recognise
intergenerational   whispering
we gather the crooked looks of others
who once were smothering us
with chocolate and softer stories.

Some stories, we might salvage
from the water where they were born
from the clay our bands once wore
from the ghosts of rusty river banks
from Tracker's forgotten paintings.

I wonder still, about his eyes
what colour, what mood were they?
To thieve from a dream or photograph
what a glance from those eyes would say?

Would they show me rivers or ghosts
    or something darker?
Would they shield more truth, or shed light
through the vines – cradle me toward
life free from tracking, of colours and freedom.

Or maybe they witnessed too much
enough to become molasses
black and thick.

butterflies

                                        time flies

blowflies

                        &butterflies

Moral Frontier I

Object Summary

Object number	88/394-1
Materials	Brass
Dimensions	Depth 9mm, Diameter 21mm
Year	1842-1856
Production	Made in Britain, United Kingdom, Europe; used in Australia, Oceania.
Physical Description	Insignia of unit on obverse, stamped, "ABORIGINES/ V.R" within garter and surmounted by a crown, belonging to Queen Victoria. Location of regiment on reverse, stamped "NEW HOLLAND" in concentric circle around edge of button.
Maker	Unknown
Owner	Unknown

Owner Occupation	Member of the Aboriginal Native Police/Native Mounted Police, circa 1840-to the turn of the last century.
Regiment	Unknown
Notes	Unknown
Public Awareness	Unknown
Significance	Is as follows; and it echoes in the memories of those descendant from brass, chains and bullets.

Moral Frontier II

If our nation's history were born of but one soldier
this badge be what was worn
without a name, needless a wage
without acknowledgement
standing beyond bronze memorials
beyond one single story.

Their nameless bodies
bore the weight of crowns
as their shadows shaped history.

Their titles are rid and forgotten
while royals remain hidden
woven deep into fabric of flags
written in names of states their work claimed:
Victoria, Wales and Queensland.

Who were these men
who rode at night
who shed tears and lead
on promised soil.

Who from quills heard promises
carried out imperial wills on horseback.

Their duty unto the crown
served but purpose for the lost
a sedative for the pain
that cannot be undone.

Invisible
may be their essence.
In memorial
is their absence.

Though their legacy
will forever be tied to our present.

Felt heavily
among the living ruins
of the survived.

What's left:
broken hearts, knapping glass,
Stolen wages paid in bullets and brass badges,
bloodstained soil, broken promises,
the unborn child's blessed inheritance:
stolen Country for them,
trauma and arsenic for the other.

Arsenic Itinerary

a lucky life
on this continent costs
a heavy dose of arsenic (As)

    (33) atomic weight of displacement
    (23) coolamons of arsenic-laced clay
    (19) brass-engraved breastplates
    (10-14) spit-hood-covered faces

    (enough) explosives swallow sacred places
– iron spears make good antennae

enough creation rock at biamanga
enough creation rock
enough creation
enough

babies belly-full of	damper
that's river mixed with	flour
mixed with heavy metal	arsenic (As)
mixed with	hands
mixed in	silence
mixed on	Country
mixed with	violence
mixed with	echoes

of asbestos / of Baryulgil

    and other skeletons

no more river
           or trickling veins
                         to clean the sap

to wash the clay

to measure the chemistry of Australia
trace genealogy of bloodlines and rivers

trace the poems and pathology
 flowing
generations of Bundjalung
         veins

observe an itinerary of arsenic
mother's stomach to woven baskets

arsenic is hard truth is
mass extinction / algal bloom

always present
    yet never spoken

        the wattle that witnesses massacre

her roots entangled in blood

or maybe it's microplastic
       swimming in our ocean

arsenic always sewn
       in every swollen occasion

arsenic through my phone
       woven in voices from home

it's in every throat
       at family conversation
family reunion / family funeral
baby showers and referendums

bodies suspended / museums
              regimes of conservation
              pesticide / preservation compound

arsenic drowns our heritage drowns
ancestors labeled ethnographic

we absorb it in silence
       like we've endured other poison

nursed hereditary bruises
       and other ongoing abuses

across our deepest ridgeline
along our softest shore

we will absorb however more
as our soil must endure

sons and daughters of tortured mothers
this be our new lore

Soil

Spear II

we
the spears
are this colony's
unrelenting burden

The Bawden Lectures I

Note: For First Nations readers, the following contains histories and events that are distressing and potentially re-traumatising.

06 July 1886, School of Arts, Grafton.

    Continuing the lecture:

"In our progress down through the heads of the Nymboy heavy rains set in, and the rivers became suddenly flooded, ██████████████████████████████████ ██████████████████████████████████ ██████████████████████████████████ in which my mother and I, ████████████ ████████████████ were conveyed across ████████ ██████████████████ waters which rolled and raged beneath.

    <u>Note</u>: In February 1843 Commander ████████ came down by Tenterfield, Tabulam and Wyan and took up Wooroowoolgen on the Richmond. From there he came to Commissioner ████████ at Red Rock and lodged his application for the ██████████████████████████ ████ ██████████████████████████████████ ██████████████████████████████████ ██████████████████████████████████ ██████████████████████████████████ country ██████████████████████████████ ██████████████████████████████████ ██████████████████████████████

on the east side of the Nymboida

He was making for Coutts' Upper Sheep Station,

The Bawden Lectures II

06 July 1886, School of Arts, Grafton.

    Commander ▮▮▮▮▮▮▮▮ letter went on:

    "Our first days journey from the Settlement (Grafton) ▮▮▮▮▮▮▮▮▮▮▮▮▮▮▮▮▮▮▮▮ us to the foot of the hills, a station of Coutts. (Kangaroo Creek) Thus far we had no difficulties to encounter.

    ▮▮▮▮▮▮▮▮▮▮▮▮▮▮▮▮▮▮▮▮ we were told we could reach the tableland in two days, ▮▮▮▮▮▮▮▮▮▮▮▮▮▮ ▮▮ ▮▮▮▮▮▮▮▮▮▮▮▮▮▮▮▮▮▮▮▮▮▮▮▮▮▮ we took only ▮ ▮▮▮▮▮▮▮▮▮▮▮▮▮▮▮▮▮▮▮▮▮▮▮▮▮▮ a little tea and sugar.

    Soon ▮▮▮▮▮▮▮▮▮▮ the weather, ▮▮▮▮▮▮▮ ▮▮▮▮▮ changed to rain, ▮▮▮▮▮▮▮▮▮▮▮▮▮▮ ▮▮ ▮▮

    "The road, ▮▮▮▮▮▮▮▮▮▮▮▮▮▮▮▮▮▮▮▮ ▮▮▮▮▮ passes through the worst country it was ever my lot to travel in, and one we should never have attempted, ▮▮▮▮▮▮▮▮▮▮▮▮▮▮▮▮▮▮▮▮

    We were constantly losing our way, ▮▮▮▮▮▮▮▮ ▮▮▮▮▮▮▮▮▮▮▮▮▮▮▮▮▮▮▮▮▮▮▮▮▮▮

████████████████████████████████████
████████████████████████████████████
████████████████████████ we had to
pass through, ████████████ rivers, or rather
torrents, all swollen very much with the rains, █████
█████

████████████████████████████████
████████████████████████████████████
████████████████████████████████

"However, we contrived to reach Coutts' upper sheep station in forenoon of the fifth day."

The Bawden Lectures III

06 July 1886, School of Arts, Grafton.

Returning to the lecture:

"The time ▇▇▇ in getting through this country having exceeded anticipations, the party almost ran out of flour, tea and sugar, ▇▇

I remember their return.

Poor ▇▇▇ was in a dreadful plight, his nose being completely relieved of skin. ▇▇▇ was a man much given to ▇▇▇ noticing a very handsome large and velvety leaf asked ▇▇ what it was.

He replied that it is the ▇▇▇ plant and has a most delightful scent when rubbed to the nose, this was his first introduction to that botanical ▇▇▇▇▇▇▇▇▇▇▇ - the giant stinging tree."

<u>Note</u>: For some years prior to 1853 ▇▇▇ worked for Mr. Ogilvie at Yulgilbar and for part of the time was in charge of the station flour mill, worked by two horses.

The Bawden Lectures IV

06 July 1886, School of Arts, Grafton.

Mr. Bawden continued:

"Kangaroo Creek was taken up by Coutts in 1840. ▇▇▇ ▇▇▇▇▇▇▇▇▇▇▇▇▇▇▇▇▇▇▇▇▇▇▇▇▇▇▇▇▇▇▇▇▇▇▇▇▇▇ The station was ▇▇ bounded on the south by Thomas Coutts' run covering the upper valley ▇▇▇▇▇▇▇▇▇▇▇▇▇▇▇▇▇▇▇▇▇▇ which took in Nymboida, ▇▇▇▇ called his station Pandemonium and ▇▇▇▇ was named Purgatory.

Pandemonium literally means "the abode of all the demons", referring of course to the ▇▇▇▇, and Purgatory no doubt alluded to the sufferings ▇▇▇ endured at their hands.

The ▇▇▇▇▇ of these parts were more aggressive and war-like than those living on the banks of the Clarence. ▇▇

The back country ▇▇▇▇ had a more direct grievance in their game being scared away and replaced by sheep. It was a matter of life and death for them.

Note: Without doubt conflicts with the blacks were more serious on Kangaroo Creek station than anywhere else in the district. ████████████████
████████████████████████████████████
████████████████████████████████████
████████████████████████████████████
████████████████████████████████████
████████████████████████████████████

████████ Besides killing his sheep and cattle the ██████ had murdered two of his men and a boy named ████████████ All this had been reported to the Commissioner ████████, but he had done nothing about it.

The Bawden Lectures V

06 July 1886, School of Arts, Grafton.

The lecture proceeded:

"There have been many instances in this district where the ▇▇▇ ruthless hand ▇▇▇ has been exercised ▇▇▇

The Kangaroo Creek tragedy may be said to have been an instance of this. You will remember that I have told you that in June 1840, the ▇▇▇ knew so little of the qualities of flour and sugar ▇▇▇
▇▇▇
▇▇▇

Huts were robbed, sheep were stolen and men were killed. It was not safe for one man to go out alone. This state of things appears to have become too burdensome.

A trap was laid for the ▇▇▇ – arsenic was mixed with flour and placed in a particular hut. ▇▇▇
▇▇▇

The thieves were traced to their camp where twenty of them were found sleeping – the sleep of death.

The ▇▇▇ perpetrators of this deed were tried, but acquitted – although the effect of it stuck to them through life.

His name remains in Coutts' Crossing.

Daam Miirlarl

Nganyundi Jaari jagun

Daam Miirlarl yilangandi biiwaywurraygam

ngirrang

My little sister's birthplace

Coutts Crossing where the massacre

happened

Root

Rise

Brotherhood is more than blood when you're the sons of tortured mothers and you're denied birthrights

                            – to have bled

for the mother.

Rise up,
                brothers.

There's Medicine in the Ashes

The institution of Man
once moved gently
like footprints in the sand
once recognised
the land held us in her hands

instead, Man now dismembers
rivers / topsoil / *himself*
tomorrow claims our attention
so came summer's intention

there's healing in melting signs
that directed us nowhere
for direction is not set by human hands
but belongs to the sun, wind and ancestors

come to know such elements
with truth and affection
surrender disenchantments
that sever land connection

next time we light a fire
we'll let Mother guide us
we'll fold dogmatic fabric
kept safe from children's eyes

signing its edges with our fingertips:
Dear Fire, we were wrong

floating new promise toward
soft, circular glow
so it be caught by hands endeared
in the shade of gentle, white smoke

may we move through burning Country
binding together tombs
singing rain, healing in hopes
that they become wombs
unearthing old spirits
in shades of the cockatoo

marked in the beginning by fire
known to bring rain
dressed in scars and sacred colours
carrying water and flame
weaving our hands together
healing through the Mother

if rains and names be now absent
let our tears water the soil
let the memory of loved ones
gild new leaves and seeds

let shaky hands turn the ashes
of **black** soil and burnt timber
so handfuls of life's remnants
meet again with fiery, **red** heat
may we recall the Dreaming
cocooning the wattle seed
may it flower **yellow** in the winter

and so observe
your bare hands amongst the Earth
you may see
there's medicine in the ashes.

Old Man's Legacy

beautiful it is
to see ochre
worn in threes

holding promises through
rain and solace
headband and posture

beautiful a legacy
reborn atop mountains
in the east

Corners

totems, both perch
as shadows on the wall

like shrapnel of our lives
they come and go with the tides

our months, paint a monet on the floor
and we rejoice in pain as artists do

corners of this room whisper
the sober part in me listens

corners trace a sovereign escapade
each other's momentary medicine

side by side, blak bodies
drown in candlelight

old flame for safety
in this century-long night

the whispers soften as walls empty
entranced in body, shadow and flame

and the corners of our room
slowly look away

runaway

actually right now

        as I stare into your brown eyes
        cradling the ends of time
        bending stars and the horizon

                for the life of me I forgot
                all the reasons why

I cannot runaway with you
to your country

Blood Cedar Dreams

blood   red
      cedar

receding dreams
of the   many
blood of the
           many legs
cut
at escarpments'
        knees

flood estuaries
        birthing
        red seas

red cedar   dreams
dead   now
blood   leaves

flowering
towering
devouring

for these pages
in your hands

                for these cages
                on our lands

Sandon Point Theory

Final Assessment (50%):

Stand on the shoulders of Sandon Point
watch the water, that which comes and goes.

Stand in the sand of my standpoint,
call it by its name: _____

Between the ochre vein
submerged old wharves
more than ancestral remains
to his status we're all dwarves.

Key Readings and Resources:

- *The White Possessive: Property, Power and Indigenous Sovereignty*, Aileen Moreton-Robinson, 2015.

- Sandon Point Theory, no date, *What Ancient Human Remains Have To Tell The Modern Fool,* by Many Elders.

- Google: *"what to do when your students are racists"*.

Shield

    o
    n
    e
   day
you'll find
yourself in a place
where people could
cut a shield from you
and you'll still be
there fucking
stand
    i
    n
    g

Aboard a Booing-37

Deadlier things than an invisible spear:
 Singing the National Anthem
 Spithoods
 The Australian Flag
 Reconciliation Cupcakes
 Fracking
 "Therapy is for pussies"
 Australia Day
 Flour laced with arsenic

Deadlier things than an invisible spear:
 Singing songlines
 The sons of tortured mothers
 The Aboriginal Flag
 The black bastard crew that won't lower their voice
 junga-ngarraanga
 Men who stand in the rain
 Yabun
 An arsenic flower

A Bowerbird for Warrawong
– *for Tyson*

A paintbrush
    your home
a paintbrush
    your throat

your wand for watersong

I watched you once

    reel in the moon
    with your bare hands

you spoke
through the paint
through your hair

    chin often resting
    in your palms

tending your gathered nest of broken objects

    a messy branch for a home

you'd flow with the rhythm
        of the city lights

     glistening against their chrome

I dream of you some nights
          flying to the moon

                  carving your nest
                  from its crevices

most beautiful atop your throne

a bowerbird with watersong
and hands glistening chrome

painting pictures with the tides

            forever shining

       moonlight, your ancient home.

Arsenic Flower

Against the pastoral grain
of kitchen floorboards,
a child is born,
in northwest Gumbaynggirr.

Bringing forward footprints and whispers
and shadows, lingering linen sheets
tethered to a clothesline –
with other domestic secrets.

More of them gather from the creek,
with love-lost ceremony, watching
a leather-skinned father, cradling
his newborn flower, mother beside him.

Heavy in his hands, a truth
warms vast silences, churns
dreamscapes singing
in wind chime tambour.

Thundering horse paddocks
could not waver their gaze,
nor could clouds of rain
forming in speech,

as trees bend to greet the unlikely
with urgent message befalling,
dancing between leaves, rising
from *biiwaywurraygam* creek;

for birth against the pastoral grain,
along this creek of unsung history,
beseeched an unsung something
between litany and eulogy,
an *old-something,* awoken, again.

From arsenic came
the privilege-burden
of memory;

of poison yet rebirth,
of people
and this Country.

Such memory spills from the soil
into the flowers and with it:

                                  promises
                                  promises
                                  promises.

For we children to hold,
to learn through echoes
of the flowers before us.

To realise our might, atop the withering
of life and ancients living within; beginning
on this verandah in ~~Coutts Crossing~~ Gumbaynggirr.

And with new birth a page turns /
truth that will heal generational curse.

Truth, that has woven pain into courage
and courage into life
and life into story
and story
into Us.

Song

Easy-Bake Reconciliation Cupcakes (makes 12)

Ingredients:
- 3 × tbsp raw sugar
- 1 × welcome to country
- 1 × cup wattleseed
- 1 × cup kakadu plum virtue
- 1 × handful of white guilt
- 1 × serve of self-raising flag
- 3 × cups of flour (arsenic-reduced)
- 3 × tsp red, blak and yellow

Instructions:
1. Preheat oven to 1788 degrees for conventional oven, 1967 degrees if using fan-forced.
2. Blend sugar, arsenic flour, wattleseed and kakadu plum virtue together in a bowl. Simultaneously, shed a few tears.
3. Slowly add your white guilt.
4. Toss in remaining ingredients and mix well.
5. Line cupcake tins with your RAP★ (12 is the preferred amount, though you may wish to reduce quantity for larger cupcakes, or increase quantity for smaller, child-friendly cupcakes).
6. Bake for 15-20 minutes, or until cupcakes are a healthy caste.

7. Allow to cool, thinking about your good-willed intentions. When you're done, decorate with lip service and share!

Check packaging for use-by date, too often RAPs are applied beyond safe consumption.

These easy-bake reconciliation cupcakes are best served with care and authenticity. Enjoy!

Spear III

To be broken / bled
stripped naked / displaced.

To meet with earth & gravel & stone
cold & wet & exposed.

To gather purpose / at the end of the world
in all its silent edges.

To nurture / protect
hands that shaped him.

To always continue
with unwavering direction.

To always return / devotedly
to Mother / his birthplace.

To know & love / with posture
this necessary plight.

Is to know the state of the spear
& the promise of he who takes it.

Nature Feels

our shadows embraced
as old friends, the night we first met

our silhouetted / moonlit / broken edges just
coalesced as such
(*mosaic*)

lining up our scars, naked in your mirror
such tectonic tasks, comforted me
(*my poetry*)

for I would spill into your cracks
just effortlessly. *mosaic* for me
to be imperfect against
(*or so I would later narrate*)

the way you would fold
the tops of your feet
across my thighs

the cadence of your hips
atop mine
like heavy rain

finding the edges,
beneath your dress
(*like pottery*)

your flowing lines
I stowed them
before I left
(*in poetry*)

(*as if your lines were ever mine to tender*)

pretending
the ground gifted me
a moment, an escape in you

when the tender thing
would have been just
to leave your shadow alone

like returning a stone
to Nature
wrongfully taken

a proclamation, I do hope
Nature *feels*
(*I am sorry*)

your body,
just an annexe
for my poetry

from your mosaic
man-made a commodity
and I did participate

for some things separate
your lines from mine:
your scars were told forevers
(*and my scars lied*)

25-to-life-type-dedication

Dedication's pressing his twenties, had his smile contentious.
Somewhere between portraits, pokies and payslips,
he's hit the minor-jackpot-black-privilege.

That's the-kettle-calling-the-pot-black-scholarship,
that's front-page-university-magazine, that's
NAIDOC-week.
All-teeth no-sleep still-black-coffee.

Three-chapters-deep, lofi-on-repeat,
thesis won't break me, no time for poetry,
don't panic, it's pay week. Too many
"*you ain't been yourself*"'s lately,
no wonder – that assessment's due, bra.

Pressures pressing his twenties, more a fear of pressure.
Fears a deeper cession lies due in his expression,
of outlandish-landless-semantics, that king's english.

Fears he's fucking up his existence,
overly-devotedly-anxious-existential-shit.

Depression pressing his twenties, fears he'll lose himself.
Fears of losing his mother to unrest, devotedly cradles, her,

unsettled-complexion painting him
a smiling-half-naked-half-caste-question-mark.

Fears of losing another brother to an entendre,
some-antics always test their patience.
So he wanders, he wonders and ponders,
resting his sentences, more comprehensive.

He's learning to keep his heart vacant, he's learning patience.
Learning that self-deprecating,
25-to-life-type-dedication.

A ventriloquising-third-person fulla.
An overly-devoted-traditional-custodian fulla.
Antiheroic-environmentalist fulla.
A not-like-the-rest fulla.
Ochred-up-gone-for-broke-shake-a-leg fulla.
A-welcome-a-week, that's rent-money-in-the-bank fulla.
Money's spent you fullas.
Sixpence, mid-twenties, ain't over yet my brothers.

SOON.
        WE.
                CAN.
                        REST.

Until then. To the young king
that prides dedication above hedonism.

Wandering, I bump into you.
The chrome of my apologetic eyes
meets yours and wonders if you ever suffer.
Pondering if doubt ever perches by your window, if so,
    how often?

Your shoulders slope so,
as if to whisper to me –

                no.
                ain't over yet my brother,
                            soon though,
                            we can both

rest.

consult to me

repetitious
tones of consulting
are weekly weakening

monotonous
acknowledgments
of country
in email signatures

traditional
custodians
must be rich,
been paid
that many "respects"

underwhelming paper-pushing
white-guilt-projecting
"Indigenous-Stakeholder-Engagement-Frameworks"
bunch of white-fulla-jargon
with dot-art-for-margins

how numbingly quick
they all are to forget
– we are in constant yarns
with past, present and future

i've devised a new
consultation framework:

        consult to me, then
        step into my land
        sing out your acronym
        stakehold my hand

    consult me, then
    undress me
    find my scars
    press on them

mark paperbark
pages on my chest
colour me in
touch me

    call me special
    acknowledge country
    reconcile me
    – a reckoning fee

        consult me then
        tear me apart
        step on my skin
        call it art

          and if i bark, muzzle me
          chain me up, disgrace me
          let me sleep, in the dark

    help me learn
    to speak in turn
    to bite my tongue
    till it bleeds

when i can't speak
i'll spit in your mouth
lend you my seat
console you, then

      i'll tighten your tie for you
      look in your eyes as you
      swallow
      the metallic truth
      in my blood

          then   consult
                  to me.

Change Direction

This is my path
I'm givin up
There's no way
I'll rise out of the pain
This is my life
I'm walkin in two worlds
I don't belong to either
Confusion and self-hate . . .
They're a part of me
I know deep down
I should be proud
I come from wisdom and warriors
Healers and storytellers
But something follows me every step I take
I know them well
Loneliness and trauma . . .
These feelings are generational
Buried in my spirit like an echo
Memories etched
From a time before mine began
This is who I am
I'm made from this hard earth
But my emotions are like rain and
Sometimes there's drought
Sometimes there's flood

My land and culture got washed away
So don't tell me
There's a power inside of me
I didn't know
Feeling lost
I'm not
Walkin in the right direction
Nah, my country tells me I'm
Voiceless
That I'm worthless
That I belong in chains
My mental health is shame
It's a lie to say
There's mob who can help me and
I can talk about these feelings
It's time to say goodbye to this life
I no longer think that
I'm gonna keep fighting
This is the moment
This is my path

↑ Now read this again – from the bottom to the top –
and see the change. ↑

Dreams

I'm sobering
to these dreams

and these dreams
are sobering to me.

Dreams
       of rivers and reeds
              of gravel and gasoline.

Dreams
       of a child who no longer
              needs to whisper their culture.

No longer will they seek refuge
in reeds or at sea.

This child rests beyond dreams
floating within our reach.

This child in you and me
is one of joy
              one of bravery.

fishing net

To be woven – like fibre
we author lives – like fishing nets.

Pinching and spinning memories
moments twirled end to end.

Instead of healing like I said I would
I'm writing this list of

                        things I'll miss the most.

How could I admit
I started twirling this –
the moment our hands first met.

              Desert-brown eyes which folded time.
                Folded dimples framing your smile.
             Skin which still held the Jawoyn sun.

Counting cars, broken glass and sunsets
from Katherine to Darwin.

                  The slowness in your breath
                – when you said my name.

Clinging
to moments.

> *The drama in that*
> *gasp, mid-laughter.*

Your presence that beaded an intimacy
toward a cosmos of endlessness
of possibilities, for two strangers –

> *The glow above your cheekbones.*

– standing end to end
we were woven anchored fibres
a patterned tension entwined.

> *The gristle toward the*
> *chewed ends of your fingertips.*

Dragging our hands through
an ocean of stars
where our fingers first met.

Cedar Creek

While you may marvel
at the stars and their beyond

        the true marvel pulses beneath your heels
                reaching for the depths in your chest.

The reason you're able to marvel at all
knows you and forgives you.

Rain

still coffee

rising from beneath the fog of sleep,
i find you in between

      the smell of chocolate and coffee
      a six in the morning ceremony

breathing life into hot water bottles
the ones not lost to a layered chaos of blankets

      across the bed / an outstretched *Morning Herald*
      your shoulders somewhere in the middle

nested between the stacks of weathered books
their coffee-stained pages vaguely decorated

      notes / feathers / letters / leaves
      all far older than me

you leave a space
by folding a corner of blanket
grandson-sized

      for my hot-chocolate-hypnotised-hands to find
      burrowing in / a scruffy note you'll attend soon

or are we just two bookmarks
in a story older than the both of us

    i try to read the news atop your palms
    noticing how different our colours are

you notice instead how cold mine are
and press on them / a newsprint-like

    confused by our contrasting hues / *interpret to me*
    (the suddenly more pressing news) / *why am I so*
        white, compared to you?

and holding this story ever so carefully
lowering your glasses as you taught me:

    Grandson

    no matter how much milk you add

    coffee's still coffee

Old Mogo Town I

It's a sore old day, when they amass, down a Princes
 Highway.
A one-horse town in Mogo, of floods and fires and gold.

With great journeys and heavy pockets, strange folk tour
 up and down.
Stepping through time, their city kind floods Old Mogo
 Town.

By the publican, masses gather, muttering 'round a post.
Pint in hand, a lawman watches. Tapping his spurs
a disdain for murmurs.
A venom, sounding like *"watch his kind"*
 spills from the foam of his drink.

Through the cold kiss of mist and bitter of charcoal
town posters discern a bushranger legend.
His face sketched from the fewest.
By the church his name condemned. His past
said to match the ash in his complexion.

And with a flare of his wrist,
one crack of his stock whip
could split the misty valley.

For the legend ranges the outskirts of Mogo
and strangers know him by whispers.

Harking across the ridge of his nose,
he fashions a bloodied bandana.
Of which he'd lower so lawmen remembered,
whispers which sang three shades of death –

a tricoloured mix of bandana, skin and toothy grin:
a haunting portrait of red, black and yellow.

On this sore old day, strangers' whispers dance 'til sundown,
when sudden silence sweeps the town. Souring every
lawman's pint, a

      DEAFENING leather-skinned CRACK of black
          lightning

cuts through Old Mogo Town.

Old Mogo Town II

The gurumbaga sung the morning
when they had him in the stocks.

His roar, enough to rattle the bolts
spurred the thought that at any moment
his horse might barrel through the crowd.

That it'd strike stiff the metal that laid him crooked
and he'd curse us all to smallpox.

For a bushranger is a bandit,
a BLACK, an outlaw. And we the innocent
outnumber them. But before his neck
would meet the gallows
he had one final confession.

For he was known
on the outskirts of Old Mogo,
and recognised a woman
in the eyes of a child.

Unholy a boy was born
with whispers as a father
wanted poster in hand
he captured the ranger's stare.

Beneath chocolate curls
– a mixed-blood crown
the boy stood out in a whitefella crowd.

From a quivering jaw
the ranger's story
lit fire to the lawman's rage.

Above the town
he fired his pistol
and with a growl
he waved the boy down.

With a dirty look
he spat on the ground
     "take a gander boy"

and saw on his face
the choice the boy must make.

With his bloodstained glove
the lawman untethered his leather
and handed the boy the bar.

    "Show the town you been civilised
    and loose a few lashes to his spine."

The gurumbaga continued to sing
while the mist came creeping in

> *"Be the hero of Old Mogo
> or join your own kind in the stocks."*

and a hundred years stood still
of floods and fires and gold.

Hunter-Gatherer

Hunt a thought

that those bits and pieces of miscellaneous curiosities
if not pried from cold fingertips
were once hungrily traded
for bags of flour, molasses and/or tea

Gather a thought

that such trades were not bereft of grievances, yet
were imbued with hope
that one day a distant grandchild would be born
with a hunger of a different sort

Hunt a thought

that although this child may grow starved of
miscellaneous curiosities
a blood-driven curiosity nonetheless,
would have them follow the echoes of those
bits and pieces across oceans' archives

Gather a thought

that cleverly cold fingertips still walk the pages of Country
and trace its corridors with cultural hunger
and blood-memory-curiosity and no longer
will be subdued by oceans, pages, poisoned flour and/or tea.

Opal

There's a nourishing silence
if you're patient
you'll find it
between the waves.

If you're listening, you're shown eternity
that deep, settled, silence.

Every emotion
in a single moment
     between
push   pull
inhale   exhale
grounded   flight

that   forever silence

beneath   the *noise.*

I was there when a train almost rearranged my journey
the blare of its horn pulled me from eternity.

By Friday my spine and shoulders ache
from carrying far too much for one tote bag
far too much for one man.

I follow the hiss of the south coast serpent
and in the rattle of its carriages
I hear the humming of the sticks
and the whitewash blending
all the noise of the world
into a push and pull
into *peace.*

The coast still calls me
coast knows when I'm sick.

The coast still sings me
home, where my spirit can drink.

Cowboys Don't Cry

I inherited many invisible things, but
your prolonged, stoic pauses *the most.*

So long they lasted,
like leather and denim,
I'd search for you in the texture of them.

On horseback adrift
your tracks like mist
into their depths – my imagination swam.

Tracing old gold mines
bracken fern and ridgelines
surveying your silent horizon – asking,

> *what stories does your heart still harbour?*

Swaying in my saddle: a laboured question mark.
I'd roam the distance between words
– disparate and unsaid – wondering

> *what rests in the depths of silence*
> *between a son and his father?*

Here I rear gently the reins,
just to see a fuller picture of him.

Wrists folded upon one another,
posture soft, yet proud,
like a king

storm-born cowboy,
(Australian-made) leather
became your skin.

Silence has brought you safety;
and what a world
you've carved from it.

How gently
you bow your head
when the track bends.

How tenderly
you draw breath
from the unsung wind.

Here in the real world, if cowboys don't cry,
this must be what they do instead.

Here in the real world, if heroes don't die,
their woes, it seems, are best left unsaid.

Best to carry them, on horseback,
in denim pockets, and leather saddlebag.

I am the son of leather and denim,
still tracing the depths to this mist.

Now I inherit the invisible things,
the secrets, the silence, the wind.

empty pegs
– *for Mum*

clothes basket bent gently against belly
hands, elbows, hips, are busy
picking at a wire clothesline

a dancing floral dress
her shadow showering daisies
sprawling her gaze, she meditates
on a kangaroo creek bed

pondering the ratio
of water to arsenic
feeding the flower
growing beneath her basket

discomfort in her toes, curling
against motherhood's doorstep

soldiering
one peg to the next

casting thoughts into blank white sheets
rolling in the breeze

soldiering
one peg to the next

a labour for her to empty
dreams, anguish
echoes from dry creek

soldiering
one peg to the next

gliding toes to heel toes to heel
swaying between shadows
soothing bruises held in soil

so like a canvas of white
against the blank she writes
a body of thoughts pendulous
surrendering them to the breeze

so she empties
into pegs, clothesline, baskets
bending labour into remedy

just as I would, later
bend poetry

empty pegs II

my mother's busy hands
once pressed
against her swollen belly
and whispered

my son
a heavy stone
you will carry in your heart
I know.

Though give yourself permission to heal
my son.

Tear these pages from their spine
surrender them
let the earth cleanse
all the stains and heavy you've kept.

Tend to them as if your clothesline, basket and pegs
your pain your memories your arsenic garden bed
tend to the pages of poetry – the stones on your chest

gather them, wash them, hold them gently
show them a river that was once empty

>   *build a tall fire to fold them in front of*
>   *birth your own flowers to unfold them in front of*

>   *I give you these gifts that helped on my journey . . .*

A handful of empty pegs,
my mother then showed me.

>   *Pass them down to the next*
>   she said
>   *and never pass them on heavy.*

Through her busy hands
the world finally made sense.

In every peg I felt her every step.
Each one that left her breathless

                                        so I could breathe.

Every time she wept in silence

                                        so I could sleep.

Every time she starved her heart

                                        so I could dream.

This labour she kept, in secret

                                        so I could live
                                        so I could leave
                                        so I could stand

– a proud flowering *something*.

So I could be a similar river or stone, to hold
                            an unbroken unspoken
                                  promise so humbly.

To me you are ancient.

You are gulaga. nardi. eve. keeper of the
                            burrow, wandaya and the
                            breeze.
                   You *are* my Country.

So in these pages, in these stains, in these sheets.
I'll sweep like you, clean like you, I'll farm for you

– amongst the frondescence of generational-story
                            from my dear inheritance
                              of arsenic and memory
from the soil, from the bruises
                      I'll harvest the essence of
                      healing-gently
just as you showed me. toes to heel. Soldiering
one peg to the next. Soldiering
one peg to the next. Soldiering
until all that's left
                    are empty pegs.

I am

I am the can they've been kicking,
instead of cleansing the soil we're from.

I am the gravel wedged under their boot,
the drought filling their gutters.

I am spear, shield, dillybag.
I am redcedar and grasstree.

I am that loose thread in their flag,
the storm where all comes undone.

I am the blinding punishment of sunlight,
now spoiling their precious view.

I am their dripping tap at night,
and other hauntingly patient echoes.

I am where their curses go,
the awkward pause in their anthem.

I am the son of the tortured mother,
emptying my chest in poems.

I am the son of leather,
and I am standing in the rain.

Born of poisoned soil and pain,
yet,
        I'm stifling them, in my power.

And,
        I am an arsenic flower.
        I am an arsenic flower.
        I am an arsenic flower.

Spear IV

△
|
|
B
E
|
|
|
T
H
E
|
|
|
|
S
P
E
A
R
|
|
|
|

Notes

SS14 + NEVILLE'S QUANTUM THEORY

Racism and Colonial Legacies

Under certain legislative acts, state governments enacted social policies to govern and assimilate Indigenous Australian populations. From a eugenicist framework of racial purity, notions of "breeding out" Aboriginal blood fuelled such policy making and the establishment of assimilationist mechanisms including Aboriginal boarding schools. A.O. Neville was a core proponent of these ideas and influenced policy and practice on Indigenous affairs nationwide during his tenure as Chief Protector of Aborigines in 1915-1920 (Western Australia).

Based on the western standard of classification of race, Neville categorised Indigeneity in a cascading series of quantums, with the underlying assumption that Aboriginality could be bred out against the mixing of ("superior") white genetics. Colonial imaginations of a "real" or "authentic" Indigenous person remain pervasive across social perceptions of Indigeneity.

Blood quantum and blood purity rhetoric are deeply traumatising as they are the very real echoes of genocidal systems dedicated to Indigenous erasure. "SS14" recalls a moment of my life, attending a university Summer School Program in 2014, when a peer asked if I was "part Abo". Although seemingly antiquated, these productions of authenticity and racial purity still colour the thinking and treatment of Indigenous people in Australia today.

Brachychiton acerifolius

Ecological Colonialism

"Brachychiton acerifolius" was produced in response to the National Herbarium of New South Wales' 1.4 million plant collection as a form of poetic counternarrative. It draws on the suspended (in)animation of pressed herbarium specimens and challenges the collection, naming and systems of classification of botany and herbaria. The Illawarra Flame Tree (*Brachychiton acerifolius*) is endemic to southeastern Australia and appears quite frequently in the National Herbarium of NSW, oftentimes identified as being poisoned by settlers and landowners.

Naming, extracting, circulating and exploiting native Australian species were fundamental objectives of early colonial botany. Productions of botanical and ecological knowledge – most often gained at the expense of Indigenous lives and labour – enabled the expansion, commodification and possession of the British over the Australian landscape, whilst disavowing Indigenous sovereignty and land-relations. The exploitation of native species for their economic, horticultural and pharmaceutical value – again, often at the expense of Indigenous lives and labour – helped enable British expansion and possession over the Australian landscape. The settlers naturalised themselves in the Australian landscape while continuing to disavow Indigenous sovereignty and land relations.

The Moral Frontier

Frontier Violence

The Native Mounted Police are, among others, an object of very few conversations documenting the history of Australian development. Predominantly across 19th-century Victoria, New South Wales and Queensland frontier history, the Native Mounted Police were organised along paramilitary lines, consisting of detachments of Indigenous troopers led by white officers. They essentially functioned to enforce the will of colonial administrators as well as protect the settlers, their livelihoods and property, and to prevent (and punish) any Indigenous aggression or resistance (see frontierconflict.org). This was often carried out through violence in many forms. Native Police were most notorious and feared in Queensland from 1849 to 1904. Similar mechanisms were deployed throughout British colonies including in India and South Africa.

"The Moral Frontier" was written in response to a Native Police Badge held in the collection of the Powerhouse Museum. For more on the Native Mounted Police see Jonathon Richards, Henry Reynolds, and The Queensland Native Mounted Police Research Database (frontierconflict.org).

The Bawden Lectures

Truth-telling and Public Memory

Coutts Crossing is a rural village located on the banks of the Orara River, southwest of Grafton. It is named after pastoralist Thomas Coutts, who settled in the area in 1840. In 1847, Coutts was accused of poisoning local Indigenous peoples by lacing bags of flour with arsenic. Twenty-three Indigenous people were murdered in this way. Coutts was arrested and tried in Sydney but was never convicted and the case was dismissed. Coutts then returned to the region and continued his pastoral activities north into Queensland.

"The Bawden Lectures" resurfaces original transcripts featured in "The First Fifty Years of Settlement on the Clarence". When Thomas Bawden was elected President of the School of Arts, it was traditional to give an inaugural lecture. He chose to speak to the history of Grafton and the Clarence District, as he had lived in the area for almost fifty years. Bawden cross-referenced historical correspondence from earlier surveyors, administrators, authorities and pastoralists in the district. The three lectures were delivered in the School of Arts, Grafton on 8 June 1886, 6 July 1886 and during August of 1886. These have been published and reprinted in several editions: 1979, 1987 and 1997. The last includes relevant historical notes by R.C. Law.

In 2018, local Anglican priest and Aboriginal Elder Lenore Parker proposed that a name change would bring unity to the region by recognising the past. Prompted by an opinion piece in the local newspaper during Reconciliation Week, a public meeting was held amongst Coutts Crossing residents to decide on whether a name change should take place. Despite historical evidence connecting Coutts to the massacre as well as Indigenous community members lobbying for a name change in the spirit of healing and truth-telling, the local residents voted a majority "no". The name Coutts Crossing remains. No formal acknowledgement or memorial to the past exists.

"Daam Miirlarl" is the Gumbaynggirr place name for Coutts Crossing, and is the site of my sister's birth, in our first family home.

Blood Cedar Dreams

Frontier Violence and Ecological Colonialism

Red cedar (*Toona ciliata*) was known as "Red Gold" by early settlers in New South Wales. By the 19th century, red cedar was Australia's third largest export, behind wheat and wool. Settlers exploited areas abundant in red cedar, including Sydney, Shoalhaven and Illawarra, until the supply was exhausted. Settlers' unquenchable thirst for red gold pushed the teeth of their saws to deep corners of the subtropical forests of NSW, then eventually QLD in the 1850s. Red cedar was highly valued for its durable, lightweight timber and its similarity to mahogany, with its rich, dark tones that marked status throughout the British empire. Its imperial allure meant that it was used in extravagant furnishings of Government House and Sydney Town Hall, promoting early Australian produce, craftsmanship and an emerging Australian nationalism.

The industry depended on the knowledge, labour, dispossession and elimination of Indigenous peoples in these areas. This commercial practice was concluded after the cedars were pushed to extinction in the 1960s. Now found in the red banisters of old bank buildings, courthouses and government offices, the once common and widespread species and exploitation of Country stands as both a metaphoric and literal foundation in the colonial nation-state of Australia.

Sandon Point Theory

Local Sovereignty and Cultural Resistance

Sandon Point, or Sandon Point Aboriginal Place, is a historic site of cultural significance for the local and surrounding communities of the Dharawal, Wodi Wodi and Yuin peoples. It was and continues to be a place of gathering, ceremony, medicine, ochre, and burials. In 1998, Sandon Point rose to public awareness after the surfacing of ancestral remains dated at 6,000 years old. The ancestor was recognized as holding significant cultural status, being referred to in local terms as *Kuradgi*.

Sandon Point presents a juxtaposing view, set against the backdrop of the growingly affluent residential and holiday destination of Bulli, a suburb in northern Illawarra. In the early 2000s, the construction of a housing development resulted in the destruction of Country, memory and evidence of ancestral occupation. A campaign to protect Sandon Point followed, including protests, extensive court cases, and state government interventions. This marked the birth of the Sandon Point Aboriginal Tent Embassy, which mobilized Indigenous and non-Indigenous local and surrounding objectors to the continued destruction and loss of heritage at the site. Due to the dedicated resistance of the local community, in 2007 the NSW Government recognized and declared the site an Aboriginal Place.

Today, this area is protected under the *National Parks and Wildlife Act 1974*.

The title is a play on Indigenous Standpoint Theory, inspired by my time teaching "Indigenous Geographies" at the University of Wollongong in 2021-22. The course – compulsory for secondary education students – involved local Indigenous knowledges and depended on students being on and with Country. Some of whom did not respond well. Hence, the struggle for cultural understanding in the arena of social and public discourse – despite our continued resistances – is ongoing and persistent.

For more on Sandon Point Aboriginal Place, see Glenn Mitchell and Michael Organ's "Re-imagining Sandon Point" (2016) and Wollongong City Council.

Shield

Modern Warriors

The words from "Shield" were given to me by a colleague and strong matriarch in the final days of employment before returning to study. "Shield" is a gesture of wisdom, kinship and support from one generation to another. Historically, our peoples have reclaimed, reordered and safeguarded spaces in all corners, peaks and plateaus of the frontier. These spaces by extension – found all across public and private sectors – are legacies of generational and cultural sacrifices. Those who have endured the complexities of Indigenous advancement and survival have amassed a large body of knowledge of the western world. These modern warriors and their *frontier knowledge* have contributed to the return of a growing wave of rights, dignities and opportunities for future generations of our people. This continued resistance has also involved producing and reproducing a set of wisdoms that seek to guide and ready the young and emergent for new and unforeseen struggles, as we have always done. We have those who came before us to thank, attribute and celebrate. So, for that, thank you, Tammy Gissell.

She-oaked shores

Caring for Country Through Poetry

"She-oaked shores" was produced for Red Room Poetry as part of the inaugural Poem Forest Project in 2021. Poem Forest is an educational poetry prize calling on students across Australia to submit poetic responses to Country and the environment. For each poem received, a corresponding tree of native species was planted on the traditional land of the Dharawal people, on Mount Annan, in the heart of the Australian Botanic Garden. It is helping restore the critically endangered Cumberland Plain Woodland and Western Sydney Dry Rainforest.

Change Direction

Mental Health, Suicide and Trauma

"Change Direction" is a palindrome poem written in collaboration with Jackson Long in 2025. The poem was written as the original monologue for a short film accompanying a public awareness campaign focused on Indigenous suicide prevention in Australia. Drawing from lived experience and the expertise of Dr Tracy Westerman from the Jilya Institute, "Change Direction" shines a light on the interconnectedness of our wellbeing and issues of identity, Country, cultural loss and trauma. The campaign launched during National Reconciliation Week 2025 and is focused on bringing attention to the systemic failure of Australia in dealing with Indigenous suicide and mental health.

The palindrome format is crucial as it can be read in both directions. This allows for two conflicting perspectives communicated through the same choice of words; only they are read in opposite directions, from different perspectives. "Change Direction" also works to make visible the silent struggle of our mob's mental health, in particular our young people. You can visit @changedirectionau to view the film, share and donate to the campaign. The funds raised will go toward empowering Indigenous organisations including the Jilya Institute in tackling suicide prevention in our communities.

Selected poems have previously appeared in other publications and initiatives.

An earlier version of "Heal Country" was published in *Overland*.

"She-oaked shores" was published in *Wonderground* and *Red Room Poetry*.

"1966" was published in *Meanjin*.

"Death by Vertigo" was published in *Rabbit Poetry* and *Best of Australian Poems 2022*.

"There's Medicine in the Ashes" was published in *SoftStir*.

An earlier version of "WRONG SKIN" was published in *10 MEN Magazine*.

An earlier version of "Consult to me" was published in *Cordite Poetry Review*.

An earlier version of "25-to-life-type-dedication" was published in *Cordite Poetry Review*.

"Brachychiton acerifolius" was published in *Plumwood Mountain Journal*. A film visualisation was produced with the support of AIATSIS and premiered at Edinburgh Festival 2022.

An earlier version of "Moral Frontier I + II" was commissioned by the Powerhouse Museum.

An earlier version of "WATER & SMOKE" formed part of an audio-visual installation commissioned by Wollongong Art Gallery. An adapted version of "Change Direction" formed the monologue of a film directed by Warwick Thornton supporting the *Change Direction* Indigenous suicide prevention campaign in 2025.

Acknowledgements

Arsenic Flower was written on Yuin, Wodi Wodi, Dharawal, Jagera, Turrbal and Lenape lands and I extend my deep respect to these communities.

Arsenic Flower could not have blossomed if not for the love, resistance and sacrifices of my Bundjalung and Gumbaynggirr mob and all my kin from Yuin and abroad. To the elders of these and other communities, I say thank you.

To my Aunty Helli and my little Sister Montana, thank you for the teaching of joy and the fact that every day on Mother Earth is a gift. To my mother, Claudia, thank you for your grace in enduring the cost and for the empty pegs. I'll never stop learning from you and your life. To my father, Adrian, my deepest fear is that I'll never amount to the man that you are. To my grandmother, Mavis, none of us would be here without you. To all my Uncles, Aunties, Nephews, Nieces, Brothers, Sisters and Cousins – I love you.

Arsenic Flower was edited by Georgia Anderson and Grace Lucas Pennington as part of the State Library of Queensland's black&write! Fellowship, a program dedicated to nurturing and supporting emerging First Nations writers.

I thank Georgia and Grace for their time, energy and care as well as extend my thanks to the black&write! judges. My deepest gratitude to Jeanine Leane, whose wisdom and experience guided me and *Arsenic Flower*. Thanks also to Bianca Valentino who proofread this work. It is a privilege to have had such an incredible network of people devote their time and energy to help me publish my debut collection. Thanks to all those who have supported me along the way. A special thanks to Charlotte Allingham, for not only the cover of *Arsenic Flower*, but for all of your creative strength that has supported me for so long. And to Kirli Saunders, Jazz Money, Jeanine Leane and Tony Birch for their voice, energy and kind words of praise for *Arsenic Flower*.

www.ingramcontent.com/pod-product-compliance
Lightning Source LLC
LaVergne TN
LVHW092047060526
838201LV00047B/1278